POEMS ABOUT ALIENS

POEMS ABOUT ALIENS

KORY VANCE

(^)

(>)

To Sacramento, the greatest poetry
city in the U.S. To the poets who came
before me. To the passion that created
the scene. To the community that
accepted me.

(<)

i was told,
this feels good, but i don't love you.

when i was abducted, the aliens asked me, chomping
  their words through heavy lips, if that's what it
  means to be human.

i said yes, a lot of the time.

(^)

(>)

(<)

Preface

Why aliens? Since starting this project in January 2022, many people have asked me this question. Most of the time, I just tell them I like aliens.

Poetry has no rules, but it often follows norms. It floats on the foaming waters that blast over icy rock. It drains into slow, thundering rivers and drifts over the salty surf of the gulf. Later, it evaporates into vapor to precipitate our gardens and flowers, growing fruit for us to consume. Largely, this flow keeps poets bound in schools. They sit cross-legged in patches of corn, wrapping zucchini vines up the tall stocks to claim a place in history.

Today, we poets tend to scrub our knuckles in grit, writing in the real world. We dissect daily experiences down to the most-shriveled appendices, swat newspapers against the tender noses of jackal politicians, and delve into the damp sand of our mattresses on days when our shoes feel too far to reach. These are important poems, and I hope my community will continue to craft them, as I intend to outside of this project. However, I've decided to escape our universe for a few pages to explore the universes of aliens.

This exploration, though, is less of a telescope and more of a mirror. My goal is to use the aliens of other worlds to explore us. How would society react? What would a person believe? Is being human the same in this world as it would be in one of theirs?

Above all, though, I want you to enjoy this book. I hope you find my writing beautiful. I hope you allow yourself to drift into somber nostalgia. I hope you laugh. —Kory

Contents

Acknowledgements

I would like to thank the following for publishing earlier versions of these poems:

Nat 1 Publishing LLC - "Fuck You With My Mother's Laser Tentacle, Frank: An Autobiography"

Gold Man Review - "Gummy Bears"

Sinking City - "Aliens Keep Hummingbirds as Pets" and "Drinking Coffee in Ankle-Deep Mud with Aliens"

I would also like to extend a special thanks to my beta readers, DeeDee Rae, Oswaldo Vargus, and Jenny Lyn, all spectacular poets in Sacramento. Thank you to M Todd Gallowglas for being instrumental in connecting me with the speculative audience. Thank you to Mario Lopez for the dope headshots in the back. Thank you to Aik Brown for pouring his heart into the original cover art.

Finally, thank you to Luna's Cafe and Juice Bar for giving space to poets since 1995. This is where the idea for the book was conceived, and where I tested the majority of poems in this book.

Introduction

Poems About Aliens is arranged into seven sections. Each represents a possible world or series of worlds where aliens interact, one way or another, with us.

We start by exploring worlds where aliens are here, but frankly, humans are far from their main concern. The next section takes us to a world of romance with three poems dedicated to a love affair with an extraterrestrial. In the third world, the poems recount an abduction. Fourth, we travel back to our world and ask if aliens are here already, how might they be guiding humans through their lives? The fifth set of worlds is full of aliens who think humans are doing life just a bit wrong, and they'd like to give us some guidance. Next, we enter worlds where money is still king. And finally, the seventh world is one where our fears are realized—a world invaded.

In some sections, the poems are connected within the same universe. In others, they are not, but each poem examines a version of a world with the same concept. These sections can be read in any order, but I do recommend reading a section in its entirety before moving on to the next. Have fun.

in worlds where aliens are
otherwise concerned

Let Me Suck The Nipple

the problem

they weren't here for us. apparently, sentient life is pretty common in the universe, and religion is as abundant as dirt. the aliens didn't even want to talk. (i mean, they didn't have mouths, but still—an effort would have been nice.) we barraged them with radio waves and homemade cupcakes like a desperate ex-lover.

> look at me! look at me!
> pick me up!
> let me suck
>   the nipple!

the aliens

these aliens had a lot of nipples. like, A LOT a lot of nipples. brown nipples, all sizes, mismatched, scattered, and random across barrels of flesh, even on their backs. their skin, like avocado leaves, was almost plastic and dark green. they had two arms but no hands. each arm was a rigid, bony jut that bent in about ten places. aliens with twenty elbows!

their legs were about eight feet long with two knees each. they wore leathery pants down to the ankles. their bare feet were more like seven-digit hands that stepped, climbed, and even pulled trees out by the roots. the aliens' weight left deep hand prints. they walked with a massive gate, making wide-arched doorways between their legs.

these aliens were headless.

the long arms were covered in eyes framed by burley lashes, probably hundreds. these eyes were always closed, though, and between them were gaping holes that sucked, making tiny tornadoes of dust. the aliens spent their days scanning the ground with their arms, lifting boulders or the foundations of old homes and waving their arms underneath.

we're pretty sure the holes were like nostrils. we think they only opened their eyes, one or two at a time, if they smelled something interesting. when they did, we saw that their arm-eyeballs looked mostly like our face-eyeballs.

but they never looked at us!

> look at me! look at me!
> pick me up!
> let me suck
>   the nipple!

the humans
several countries, my america most of all—engine of pork, corn, and bad tinder dates—established special branches of military to monitor the aliens. one country blasted a nippled alien with a bomb (i'm not, not saying it was north korea.) didn't even knock the damn thing off balance.

christian evangelists wore patagonia wind breakers and followed their assigned alien for months. churches in the network of god's soldiers had rallies to supply peanut butter sandwiches to these men and women doing the lord's work. the evangelists read scripture to the aliens and tried teaching them to pray. the towering aliens had no hands to fold. they sniffed the peanut butter, but didn't so much as squint an arm-eye a centimeter open at the humans.

a few daredevils and homeless folks hung hammocks between the alien legs, roamed with 'em, saw the country.

billionaires bargained, offering gold, even offering their wives, for a ride to space.

the goddamn hippies protested, saying the aliens deserved privacy. they advocated for modesty covers, bed sheets WE WERE SUPPOSED TO DRAPE OVER OURSELVES so we couldn't watch them, couldn't disturb the aliens on their "journey." said it was wrong to photograph or video, too. they even value-signaled by throwing their camera phones in the trash and setting the trashcan on fire, yet somehow still managed to post the burnings on instagram by the thousands.

the farm workers couldn't be bothered. the harvests were smaller, for the massive handprints upturning roots. the workers had to cover more ground to keep our families (and their families) fed.

baristas continued being vegan.

bartenders listened to the exact same number of stories about how the world is ending and that the government did it.

economists predicted inflation and said that the government did it.

eight-year-old boys in shorts and crocs scuffed their feet across the sidewalk to inch closer-closer-closer-inch-closer and poke, just barely poke —eyes wide and nervous above a cheeto-crumb-smile—just poke the alien leg.

there were a few romantics, the ones really into nipple play, who thought they were falling in love with the aliens. they waited for cloudy nights, lightless as sin, and naked-rubbed their nipples on the nipples of disinterested aliens.

the sightings of priests trying to plug the aliens' arm-holes with their penises were alarmingly higher than even the most dejected of former-catholics would have guessed.

but no matter what, they wouldn't open their damn eyes!

> look at me! look at me!
> pick me up!
> let me suck
>   the nipple!

the solution
we tried everything!

we made signs,

and we flashed strobe lights,

and offered our virgins against their crying will,

and we poked the aliens with the pokiest sticks,

and we spoke to them with representatives from the united nations in every conceivable language (feminists pointed out that this should have been attempted prior to offering virgins),

and even our scientists called on shamans in peruvian alpaca hair to dose them with frog slime,

and a fourth grade teacher tried a talent show,

and we fucking cried into the void of the universe—ripped open our souls —shaved our heads and covered each other's genitals with burlap—vowed to silence,

and the CIA recruited our very best porn stars, and hollywood directors, and bollywood directors, and a DJ, and laser light technicians, and freestyle drone operators, and acrobats, and a big fat man telling jokes, and a pretentious french woman smoking a cigarette, and a burning hulahoop with a goldfish to jump through it, and bellows of artificial smoke, and good, down-to-earth, hairy thespians, and we put on the greatest goddamn show the world will ever see!

and the aliens wouldn't open their stupid eyes!

> look at me! look at me!
> pick me up!
> let me suck
> the nipple!

the mission

on occasion, a worm would pop out of the soft soil after a night rain. on occasion, a hedgehog would roll on its back and yawn, lazy and long, to take a belly-up nap. on these occasions, and only on these occasions, the aliens opened a single arm-eyeball to watch.

Aliens Keep Hummingbirds As Pets

My mother always kept a mummified hummingbird in her china cabinet. It was entombed in a glass box with tarnished brass corners, smaller than a deck of cards. The china cabinet's glass was thin, and it curved between the varnished, cherry frame. That Kentucky antique was responsible for my family's blood pressure, pulsing like bowling balls through a water hose every time we moved homes.

Don't let it break! Don't let it break!

We moved every few years. My family replaced hugs with trips to the grocery store for banana boxes and packing tape. I can't remember hugs from my parents. I'm sure they would have happened, though. I think growing up was a bit like army crawling under a tissue paper blanket suspended eight inches above the carpet, and the world will end if the paper rips.

Oh well, humans don't live so long, anyways. That's how ZZZZXCHRT sees it.

Also kept in the china cabinet was an almost-complete set of yellow depression glass, which is see-through, glass tableware that used to be included in food packages during The Great Depression. Mom collected it, and, despite scouring all the flea markets along Tornado Alley, she was still missing the gravy boat and a sugar jar. My Royal Rangers trophy for winning a match car race was also there, along with some Garfield drinking glasses from the '70s.

ZZZZXCHRT, when they first came to Earth, was fascinated by the cabinet's contents and spent hours examining each piece. Most of all, they loved the hummingbird. It made them cry steaming tears that fogged the glass.

Aliens keep hummingbirds as pets. They use our planet as an incubator and aviary. XXKRRRKRK originally introduced hummingbird eggs to our planet about thirty-million years ago, along with gnats and cardinal flowers. They did not expect creatures with moral agency (humans) to evolve here.

Every year, thousands of hummingbirds are abducted for the intergalactic pet trade. They are dying now. I sometimes try to impress my dates with how many facts I know about hummingbirds. I'm still single.

The birds are dying. ZZZZXCHRT is here to investigate. They heard of my mom's hummingbird, the only-ever mummified hummingbird. That's how we met.

They asked me, while standing on a chair to be at eye-level and chirping from their beak into an interpreting machine, if she preserved the body because it had been her pet. I said no, but when I was a child, Mom did keep a stillborn goat and a dead hamster in our freezer for three years. She kept the baby goat to bury with the goat mother, who, for years after the still birth, hobbled around shedding cacao fur in the corner of her dusty pasture, away from the other goats. Eventually, she leaned-leaned-leaned over dead in the dirt.

(As a side note, I had another goat named Abigail get eaten by a dog. She had been very affectionate. Her daughter, Windy, later got her head caught in a fence and broke her neck. My family never had so much luck with goats.)

No one knows why Mom kept the dead hamster for so many years, wrapped in a pinch-sealed sandwich bag behind boxes of fish sticks, and I felt too weird to ask. It had died of old age before we even had goats, but it was also buried with the goat family. In my family, we could be reprimanded for laughing too hard or too much.

We also don't know why she kept the hummingbird. When Mom was a small child, it died flying into the window of her family's Kentucky home.

She put it in a glass box, and the box turned out to be air-tight, so the carcass didn't rot. Fifty years later, I think she's just seeing how long it will last.

Her mother, my grammy, is breathing bleach and wandering the halls of a small-town nursing home. There are other people with her now, in her Alzheimer's mind—children needing her care and short people living in trees. Grammy keeps eating. We do not know how long she will last.

Are humans preserved in glass? ZZZZXCHRT wants to know. No, we burn our dead and turn them to ash. In fact, my dad's parents, Grandma and Grandpa, we kept their ashes in a closet for eighteen months because the trip to the family graveyard in Iowa was too expensive. We eventually got them there.

Hummingbirds are the only birds that can fly backwards. Hummingbirds weigh less than a nickel. Pesticides are killing the hummingbirds. Hummingbirds sleep hung upside down. House cats are killing the hummingbirds. Hummingbirds cannot smell, walk, or hop, but they have excellent eyesight. Red dye is harmful to hummingbirds. Hummingbird wings flap over fifty times per second. When hummingbirds migrate, they fly over the entire Gulf of Mexico in one go. That means on this trip, they flap their wings around 2.75 million times. Habitat loss is killing the hummingbirds. Hummingbird tongues can move in and out of their beaks thirteen times per second, potentially making them the most naturally-gifted creatures at cunnilingus, though this has never been observed in the wild or in captivity.

ZZZZXCHRT's report on hummingbird mummies as a potential threat to their species was inconclusive. They told me when I die, they would like to put me in a glass box, also, to remember our time together.

Lullaby

if an alien whispered a lullaby,
its breath would smother
the flames of our candlelight,
and the flicker-flicker
of little hearts would rest

oomh

oomh

oomh

and the flicker-flicker
of little hearts would rest

oomh

oomh

oomh

we need the sleep—sleep that's sweet like maple leaves, soft and spongy,
we could sink into and breathe softly—where the purple night blankets us
in clean air—with the weight of lead—the touch of lamb's ear—cool like
midnight grass sssssssssssssssssssssssssssssssssssssssssssoomh oomh oomh

k oomh

ooo

oomh oomh

kumph!

oomh

oomh

oomh

kumph! k- kumph! kumph! oomh

psst!

psst!

psst!

psst!

psst!

psst!

psst!

pssssssssssssst!

pssssssst!

pssst!

psst! psssssst! psst! psst!

but where are the aliens when revivals don the white or black robes of
revolution, and we the people in droves scorch our palms with candle vigils
and torches? to dawn! to dawn! we'll work 'til dawn! we'll march 'til dawn!
we'll scream 'til dawn! or in the evening calm, we'll linger in the salvation of
gin, or fishnets and glow sticks, and just for a while forget to a

beat

b-beat

stomp!

beat!

stomp!

beat b-beat stomp!   beat!   stomp!

beat b-beat stomp!

stomp!

beat!   beat!

beat b-beat stomp!   stomp!

kumph! gk psst! psst! gk k-psst! kumph! kumph! gk psst! gk k-psst! kumph! psst! kumph! gk! kumph! k-kumph!   kumph! k-kumph! gk psst! psst! kumph! gk! kumph!

beat b-beat stomp!   beat b-beat stomp!

stomp!   beat!

and for a while forget to a

beat

b-beat

stomp!

beat!

stomp!

beat!

psst!

gk

psst!

Stomp!

gk

gk

beat!

Stomp!

psst!

beat!

beat!

gk

gk

psst!

Stomp!

Stomp!

psst!

Stomp!

when an alien hums our lullaby, we won't be ready. we haven't brushed our
teeth yet, and the room's kind of hot. we are in bed watching youtube and
won't let the light dim out—no one told us "good night, sweet dreams!"
but we need sleep. the tomatoes still need watering, and paying rent
depends on the economy. no one washed the sheets, and the screeching
sirens tingle in our skulls like thumb tacks on the dashboard. the hippies
are marching with cardboard and kazoos. but the guns aren't aimed at
them. and my cousin stole her daddy's gun and traded it for drugs. she
keeps making babies. and in the world, grubby babies hobble over glass
and grime in bare feet, and most of 'em gulp sugar and chomp cafeteria
peanut butter with rotting teeth, and some don't eat on the weekends. and
my other cousin dropped his baby down the stairs, and it had to have
surgery on its head, and most of my family are racists, and i'm on the run
from everyone, held up in the backseat of a car down a meth-running road,
sweating in the summer heat. and i haven't cried sober since i was fifteen,
but we need sl—the bedroom is beige and we always wanted it bright, neon
green with ferns and lava lamps, and parents who say i love you. we need—
no one checked for wolves, or monsters, or even shut the door, or built a
door with a lock, or built a door at all, or cut a tree for lumber, or planted
the tree, but we need sleep...

but

but

ut

ut

if an alien sang a lullaby, it would go like breathe breathe breathe breathe breathe breathe breathe breathe oomh breathe breathe oomh breathe oomh breathe breathe oomh breathe ut oomh breathe oomh breathe ut oomh breathe oomh ut breathe breathe oomh ut oomh ut breathe oomh breathe ut oomh breathe ut oomh breathe oomh ut breathe oomh breathe ut oomh breathe oomh

and the flicker-flicker
of little hearts would rest

                    oomh

          ut

                oomh

              and the flicker-flicker
              of little hearts would rest

                                  oomh
                                      ut

                                oomh

in a world where i fell in love

Rabbit Pies

Written July 12th, 2022 (four months later)

The Ladybug:
A ladybug landed on my knee and said, "You know, you know, God never called you sexy." I'm a big boy, so I didn't cry or anything. We just sat there a while and talked about the weather, about how it makes the flower heads too hot. And then I asked what the ladybug knew about God.

The ladybug listed these facts:

1. "God and Darwin found similar things to be quite sexy."

   (When I told the ladybug I've only slept with eleven people, which is about one per year or less, it laughed and said, "I would have guessed fewer!")

2. "God made the Earth, and it was much like your grandma making pie dough. The ingredients were simple, but difficult to mix the right way."

   (Pie dough is salt, water, frozen butter, and flour, all just enough, pulled with the same fingers that pressed cold on your eight-year-old neck when fixing your shirt collar for church.)

3. "God only gave one defense to rabbits. It was reproduction: lots of sex, short gestation, and large litters."

   (So, both the earth and grandma's crusts are filled with rabbit meat. It tastes so sweet when baked with cabbage.)

The Alien:
later that day
       i met
       another lady
           a lady maybe
               from outer space

she had green lips
       glass skin
           and her skin
               was a window
                   to a heart
                       full of grace

               we laid on the river banks
                    on our backs
                    to watch the sky

          yes, we became lovers!

               touching shoulders
                on blanket
                    with a cooler
                       full of rabbit pies

Memphis, Tennessee **1**

She asked me, "Do you know what God calls sexy?"

I answered, "It must be survival. Why else the decay?"

"Survival and what else?" she replied.

"When the caterpillars eat plastic. Or when mushrooms grow in crude oil."

"Yes! And also survival in space."

New Orleans, Louisiana

She pleaded, "But dream of the cities. Dream of the cities, in all the new galaxies, we'll see."

My alien lover asked me to leave with her, when the spring turned fresh, when the peach trees just grew leaves.

It was a shitty time to tell her I loved her.

She asked, "When the world turns to dust and we run out of rabbits, will love be enough if we stretch it with cabbage?"

---

1 this alien was a bohemian and
came to see our cities.
she said a world before its end
is what she finds so pretty.
we went around the
world, sipping coffee
on every famous street.
i paid for the best hotels
selling pictures of her alien feet.

The City:
in the morning the alien was gone

i walked out for a coffee and saw
        a woman in a moldy t-shirt
                and crocheted shawl
                screaming, "you ain't shit!"
                                to no one at all

this woman, on the world of my birth, the dirt i've called love, barefoot
prostitute, scabs on elbows, head-ticking addict, wrenching hunger inside a
kingdom's surplus of bleached flour

                i gave our leftover rabbit pies
                            to the woman screaming
                                not a woman, even

but a messenger from god²

and she's pretending
        she needs saving
                with charity lunch plates
                        because the gesture is kind
                                and there's hope in the gravy

        and then her screams are a song!
                she's our angel with a lyre!
                        i want my world to have a home
                                i sleep like rocks on fire

The City:
in the morning the alien was gone

2(i want that to be true so badly)

Glass Angel

Written March 1st, 2056 (many years later)

when i say she had glass skin
i mean it was transparent
and changed colors by the time of day
golden with crystal flakes
on a sunny noon
and in a cloudy dusk
she turned balmy and blue

i mean that her skin was smooth
and i could glide the heel of my hand up
her thigh, through the mountain fog that
swaddles young lovers, hardening them
into fossil relics to be held in reverence
by patron saints biting their lower lips

i still dream about the nights
she held my head on her bare stomach
with a deep magenta hue
under a hazy quarter moon

now i am old with failure and cracked hands

i stayed here!
i championed revolutions!
tamed the bureaucracy and molded
governments in our image—i housed all
my neighbors, and the schools have better books
but the dust still came

sometimes i drive my van
deeper into the desert
where the city's scattered grit—
rust of fuel tanks—powder of bricks—
cannot block the stars

i watch them and trace
new constellations
in the shape of a glass angel

Don't Think About It And Say Yes To Everything

Written March 17th, 2022 (one day before)

hold onto me
through spring
so we can pick
fresh peaches

i once asked a 60-year-old dishwasher
named ron if he had ever
accidentally dated someone who
was in a different country

    he said yes
    that's happened to me twice

i asked him what i should do

    he said don't think about it and say yes to everything

        the thing is
        i knew that was true

    "truth" is chasing rabbits bathed in canola oil

all our scholars and hawaiian shirt day drinkers and artisan pork rind-
crusted-podcast-aficionados have debated their lives away about whether to
wear rubber gloves or catch bunnies bare-handed

                    speaking for me, in spite of every
                    greasy rabbit stuffed in my pockets
                    i said no to going to south korea
                    with that woman

                                        that was five years ago

now that i'm in love again
i see the speckled rabbits
cookies and cream
bouncing in the clover

                              now that i'm in love again
                              i can hear the rabbits scream

        they scream like people (children really)
        innocent and through buck teeth

this lover's body is glass and shattering—
she is rain and golden ringlets
refractions of cloud-filtered light, glimmering
shaded denim in the dusk where we were first naked—
where i bit her collar and she pressed my shoulders into the river sand—
her green lips on my neck

        this lover, too, asked me to leave today

                    this time in a rocket to be
                    wrapped with her in the stars

                              but the peach trees
                              just grew leaves

in a world where i was
abducted

Abducted

i was told,
this feels good but, i don't love you.

when i was abducted, the aliens asked me, chomping their words through
  heavy lips, if that's what it means to be human.

i said yes, a lot of the time.

(^)

black lights soak into scars, ghosts of barbed wire and asphalt
hearing the metallic shimmer of saws and violins
floating flower petals in sticky liquid
dust drifting in puppet strings of sunlight that dangled through sheer
  curtains in a dim room where the tables are covered in lace
smelling gasoline in a rosebush
a worm is afraid of the dark and dries in the sun
this is our world!

scraping fat and meat off animal skin, not knowing if the ones you will
  keep warm with your pelts would hold your tired forearm otherwise
this is our world!

(^)

when i used to sleep outside, trembling in my hammock, the winter's chill
  lingered, unwelcome, in the spring midnight. a man born of dirt and black
  walnuts, i was hidden in the woods, with my motorcycle hidden nearby.

there were nightmares before i had seen a monster. dead coyotes
   animating, taking from my flesh. in the nightmares, their eyes would glow
   like flashlights.

but there were no lights in the abduction, only warmth, an instant change
   of there to here—dark to void—alone to lonely—fear to helpless.

but their hands were warm, taking my clothes that were soaked in forest
   dew and wrapping me in their quilt, soft as breath.

(^)

they were only curious.

i told them that, on our planet, from the subject's perspective, there is no
   meaningful difference between curiosity and sadism.

they could not understand, but wanted to.

i said, i only know what i've been told.

i was told by a pastor that rap is sin.
i was told by a teacher that history is war.
i was told by a woman that blowing into a vagina will cause death by
   aneurism.
i was told by the government that i'm safe from missiles.
i was told by my mother i hated math.
i was told by my grandfather that we are free.
i was told by a hippy to be gentle with myself.
i was told by a lover nothing, just silence.

(^)

but of these things, what do you feel?

i said i feel like wedging myself between bodies and cushions when the
   wind is cold, threatening rain.

Glass

when the aliens asked me to explain respect, tears drained from my eyes—
   the sweat of a laboring soul.

the gravity was strong, and my fluid dropped like anvils to the hardwood
   floor of their vessel.

yeah, it turns out alien ships are made of wood. who would have thought?

also, no probes. they aren't nearly as interested in asses as humans. they
   had asked me about that, too, but when i tried to explain, i couldn't.

i told them all i know of respect is that i treat my body and soul like hushed
   pink cherry blossoms in a painting, the ones we know are delicate but
   never break-flutter-fall in the wind.

i've been told i have the respect of my peers in friendship and in business.

but in solitude, my tendons strain against barbell steel, denying promises
   made by gravity to the rubber floors.

when marble sheds tears for its sculptor, it wants to have earned its shape.

my soul is built from old light bulbs with thin glass,

each hung half an inch apart by thread.

i build around it my muscles—bulk—mass—

i will not shatter.

i will not shatter.

i stand in stiff breath under hundreds of pounds of weight—

i will not break.

i will not break.

Rattle

nothing I want more
than to brush the backs
of hands with strangers
and be strangers no more

i sit cross-legged with the aliens and we discuss the matter.

they tell me that, on their planet, skin is knit by one mother, different
  textures and colors, but all from the same spool of yarn.

every alien can hold hands with every other alien because it's like holding
  their own hand.

they each lay a three-fingered hand on my torso, covering my shirtless body
  from chest to pelvis.

their hands have weight and feel like water balloons wrapped in warm
  velvet.

my new friends flap their fleshy lips, filling the room with pops and clicks.
  somehow, i understand them.

they want to know about us—not what we are, but how we touch.

(^)

on the spot!
now it is me
speaking for humanity!

it is me who sometimes stands alone in swamp moss while thinking of my
  people.

my people who stand for miles on river rocks
side-by-side with arms outstretched
almost touching knuckles—each hand
gripping an aluminum can
half full of dried beans
                and shaking,

just not always on the same beat.

it is us—us with feathers hidden behind our eyelids,
never flew—never flew—never stopped wanting to—and won't put up
  with the bullshit.

it is us, hand-digging pits
to plant peach trees
and weaving grass into baskets
and filling them with honey bees
and saving the world
with budgets on excel spreadsheets
and smiling just to see
if we feel like smiling.

(^)

i tell the aliens about a homeless man who always smiles.

he gave me a fist bump at a bus stop.

a woman with a big ass walked by wearing yoga pants.

after she passed, he jumped up and down in excitement, muffling his
  words, "do you see her?!"

i thought to myself, "he's goddamn right."

i tell the aliens, "ya know, we don't touch so much, but we thank our good
  god in heaven for yoga pants!

we praise the scientists who work out that stretchy technology, ignoring
  cancer and climate change!

it's what we are! it's what we are! i can't help it! we look at people in yoga
  pants and have to be quiet about it!"

(^)

the aliens smile and say

it is you, all three of you, all three the same
you, the woman with the big ass, and the smiling man
you are standing on the round rocks of a dry river bed

now build a raft with tiny, black cocktail straws
                              big enough for you all
        wait for the rain to
                rattle-rattle
                    on the rocks

in my world

Fuck You With My Mother's Laser Tentacle, Frank: An Autobiography

First, let's discuss cosmology. Gather around, please, to hear the creation story for you and the universe.

It was aliens.

We are living in the equivalent of their sandbox. I should tread lightly, seeing as they could shut out the lights at any moment, but if you ask me, the aliens are shits. In the entire universe, they only managed to make life on Earth, and if we are being honest, it was a complete accident.

Frank was daydreaming while pumping the gas into Saturn, and it got away from him. Saturn is way, way too big. Then, while Janice was slamming Frank's head in a freezer door over and over as punishment for the mistake, all the asteroids were slung away from Earth by Saturn's gravity, and we got to keep our atmosphere. So then there were single-celled organisms, and then there were fish, and then the fish grew legs, and so on and so on.

Frank and Janice couldn't believe it. They immediately started tinkering to take back control, but they were not great at that either, especially when humans came along. We kind of do our own thing, but the aliens want us to do their thing.

When we make cultures, it is similar to making grooves in stone. What I mean by grooves is that, if you're born into a Christian conservative family, you are likely to stay a Christian conservative. If you are born into a Muslim family, you are likely to remain Muslim. If you are born into a hyper-liberal family and are taught shoes are of the devil, when you grow up, you're likely to teach your unvaccinated kids to brew kombucha. And so on and so on.

Frank and Janice like to keep us in our respective grooves because that makes them feel in control. If they use their tentacles, they can hypnotize us to a point, and that's how they try to keep us in line. When someone falls out of their groove, it's usually because Frank and Janice made a mistake. Honestly, if they stopped trying to keep people in the grooves, everyone would probably stop falling out altogether. As I said, they are shits.

Here's what happened to me.

I was born in Southeast Missouri to a Pentecostal family. When Frank put one of his tentacles in my brain, he leaned in too far. Frank snorted up a bunch of pesticides from the soybean fields, which made him sneeze. The jolt seemed to turn my brain into a bad brain.

Janice still had curlers in her tentacles when it happened. She yelled, "Dammit, Frank! Fucking dammit! You fucked it up, Frank! You fucked up the gray matter real good this time, Frank!"

Frank returned, "Get off my fucking back, Janice!"

Frank sneezed again, chemicals still up his snout.

What proceeded can only be described as domestic violence in outer space, but it's not as bad as you think. They dish it out equally and take it easily. While the pots and pans were flying, all the jumbling helped me slip out of the groove. So, despite my conservative commitments, I realized it was okay for my friends to be gay.

"Fuck you, Frank!" screamed Janice.

"Fuck you around the corner, Janice!" screamed Frank.

"Fuck you with my laser tentacle, Frank!"

"Too far, Janice!"

"Laser right up your reproduction hole, Frank!"

"Why do you always go there? You know how sensitive I am!"

"Sensitive in your reproduction hole, Frank!"

"Fuck your mother!"

About the time Frank said "fuck your mother," his tentacle finger twirled around in my brain again. That unblocked some more knowledge, and it's how I realized most of my beliefs came from pulpits and aliens. I started spending more time with people different from me.

"Frank!" screamed Janice. "Fuck you with my MOTHER'S laser tentacle!"

"You would never take it out of the urn, Janice."

"I fucking might! Look at him! He's going rogue!"

"This happens sometimes, Janice," Frank took a breath and sat down. The alien looked into Janice's eye and continued calmly, "Perfection is an impossible standard. We must be inwardly gentle and forgiving of ourselves. Mistakes are a part of life."

Janice threw every limb and appendage in the air and screamed, "They're a pretty fucking big part of life when you're involved, Frank!"

"Oh, like you've never made a mistake!"

"You're a fuck-up, Frank! A big, fat fuck up!"

Janice shoved Frank's fourth head inside a black hole, and Frank saw things that I really cannot repeat in polite company. While Frank was screaming for a few hundred millennia in another dimension, his tentacle flinched quite a lot, and made me realize there are not a whole lot of differences between all the world's religions.

Frank finally pulled out of the black hole and yelled, "You're a bitch, Janice! You're a pot roast-burning, ball-busting, tight-ass, gigantor bitch! Bet you'll blame me for this shit, too!"

"You're fucking right about that one, Frank! Look at what you make me do when you fuck up! This is what happens when you fuck up!"

"Cunt!"

Frank lost his shit. He tore out Janice's only eye and wolfed it down with a big glass of milk. While that was happening, his tentacle slipped out of my brain completely. I was just doing my own thing for a bit, and it became obvious that rich people run everything.

Shortly after, Frank and Janice received an email from Goldman Sachs. The email simply read: NO MORE BLOWJOBS.

Frank mumbled, "Uh oh."

"What was that?" Janice demanded.

"Nothing."

"Jesus Christ!"

"He's not here," Frank whispered.

At this point, Frank stuck his tentacle back in my brain, but it was way too fast and rough. I started to think maybe there isn't a god at all.

Still blind, Janice asked, "Where's my blowjob?"

Frank stayed very quiet.

I began drinking a lot.

Janice said, all suspicious, "Frank…"

"What?" Frank responded, trying to sound confident.

"When my eye grows back, I better not see anything I don't like. Are you fixing the gray matter?"

That angered Frank, and he got all childish, balling up his tentacle into a fist inside my frontal lobe. I started dating girls who made me feel empty and numb. I stopped praying. I stopped helping my community. I even stopped writing.

Janice's eye grew back, and she saw the email.

"Fuck! Fuck!" Janice screamed in a panic. "Fuck Frank! No more blowjobs, Frank! They said we don't get no more blowjobs, Frank!"

Frank responded, "Well, you pushed me!"

"I'm about to blow, Frank!" Janice yelled with her baby eye bulging out.

"It's not my fault you can't keep it up your shoot, Janice!"

"I swear to Jesus I'll blow it up your reproduction hole, Frank!"

"I told you, Jesus isn't here!" Frank whined. "He went out for cheeseburgers."

Janice looked down through her wiggling knees and screamed, "Frank! He's all fucked up, Frank!"

Janice thrust her tentacle into my brain, trying to knock Frank out of there. Nobody was wearing condoms, and the whole affair was quite a lot. I don't know if the result was good or bad, though it's likely not meaningful enough to matter. I gave up, got rid of everything I owned, moved to Hawai'i without enough money to buy a return plane ticket, and broke up with a girlfriend over the phone after landing. The drinking started again.

Janice stuck her tongue out at Frank. Frank crossed his eyes at Janice.

I decided I didn't want to get married.

Frank screamed, "I don't even know why, but that bothers me!"

With her head down, Janice said, "Just take some napkins and wipe the whole fuck'n thing up."

I almost died in a couple of motorcycle accidents, another time with my back to a boarded-up door in a meth house, and a few times from food poisoning and too much alcohol. There was also the time I was mildly kidnapped in Arizona.

Janice screamed at Frank, "Don't just throw the napkins down on the floor and push them around with your foot! Bend the fuck over and get it all, you lazy, fucking asshole!"

Frank burst, "For the love of Christ!"

Jesus responded, "What was that?"

Janice perked up and asked, "Did you bring the cheeseburgers, Jesus?"

Jesus passed a bag of cheeseburgers around before leaving. Frank and Janice stuffed them down their feeding holes. It made them feel a little better, but while their attention was off me, I voted for Bernie.

"Dammit! Dammit! Dammit! Dammit!" screamed Janice.

Frank inched away.

"Don't you run away, asshole!"

"Fuck you, Janice," Frank whispered.

"It's your fault, Frank! It's your fault I'm about to blow, Frank!"

I then realized hippies, too, are out of their fucking minds.

"Don't blow!" screamed Frank. "We're too close; he won't be able to come back from that much exposure!"

I now believe everyone is a little out of their minds.

"I'm gonna blow!"

"DON'T BLOW!"

No one has a monopoly over truth. Take things less seriously. Play around and smile.

"Ahhhhhhhhhh," Janice screamed.

Janice blew.

in worlds where aliens have advice

Butterfly

when i thought that, i was lying on a boulder up mount chilhowee and bedded down for sleep. the mountain fog swarmed, stinging my nose with freezing pricks. the stars were a dusty smear of giants' eyes peaking through the shadows. my eyes locked on one star as it began to flutter, shimmering silver and gray. the glimmer grew bigger, and its fuzzy halo transformed into legs and antennae. it had wings that glowed neon blue. the star was a butterfly.

the butterfly floated all the way from another galaxy to whisper in my ear, "it's true, you are alone. very alone. so alone. in fact, the most alone anyone has ever been. what a loser!"

the butterfly told me that it can give dreams by landing on a forehead and flickering its wings. i asked for one:

maybe with the woman where
we're in a mountain cabin
mixing chocolate in our porridge
roasting ducks stuffed with oranges
wrapped in blankets by a midnight fire

the butterfly responded, "that's pathetic. i'm not doing that. you already know she'll never love you. but i will give you a dream where you can act like, you know, a man. say your peace and all that shit. should be fun for me to watch! didn't come all this way for nothing..."

and then there was sleep

we stood there
in the hot, dank air
between chipped bricks
that stacked endlessly into buildings
with no doors or windows
        they rose
                so high, we could not see
        their roofs in the dishwater smog

"go ahead and say it!" thundered the voice of my extraterrestrial insect-enchanter.

the sound shook blue birds and cardinals
from their nests in the brick
frantic, colorful streaks churned through the haze
feathers rained from the cloud
a red feather landed on my love's left shoulder
a blue feather planted in her walnut hair

the woman who bounced when saying hi
her smile was made of ghosts
laying hands on the freshly-bathed child
legs stuffed in pajama shorts
too afraid to ask for a hug

she waited politely, eyes glancing
to the side, and one ankle
crossed over the other
standing on a crack in the concrete

i cleared my throat and said, "let me take you
away from here, to a place where it rains
to a place with seashells on the river banks

to raft a river through the forest
> *where goblins and gremlins*
>> *hum the songs of justice*

to teeter the waterfall
> *on earth's edge and drift*
> *through galaxies*
>> *to planets with mollusks*
>>> *that bathe*

> *in dying starlight*
> *eating sand to gestate*
pearls for a great empire in space
> *still millions of years away*

and then let me take you back

> *to the heart of my home*
>> *where we chew wheat heads like gum*
> *and pick plums*
>> *in the shade*

>>> *i want your palm*
>>> *on my knee*
>>> *i want to take you*
>>> *where it rains."*

when i woke up, the butterfly was resting on my forehead. its wings were popping and sinking rhythmically like the hydraulics were failing.

it said, "well, that was fucking dramatic. no wonder you're alone."

Drinking Coffee In Ankle-Deep Mud With Aliens

the fuzzy, pink aliens came, and indeed they had lips, thick like zucchini
and soft like the belly of a puppy, all slobbery, too, smacking together
when they spoke

the aliens told us you birthed your god in coffee steam and asked what is all
the fuss about?

we said, we just have so many tasks!

indeed the aliens had softball-sized eyes

they told us, we see your task

your task is in the jelly-legged ranks of steel-toed society, kicking your
swollen feet through the sludge and hauling quarry stone with crackling
finger bone—building the high-rises where kings are buried

your task is where scabby hands pour oil into pumps that suck gunk out of
drinking water—spilling hydraulic fluid the whole time

your task is in avoiding eye contact on the street—your eyes crossed into
one another—bloodshot and clotted with dying

your task is in squishy lungs inhaling volcano sunsets and nuclear fog

your task is families collapsing on knees—shivering in the rain—hungry—
praying for horsepower and grain

your task is sinking in the sloppy earth—screaming gurgles to seismic
  detectors—making the last plopping bubbles to be heard by heaven

your task is in the mud

indeed the aliens had big bellies and met us with hugs

they told us, you have to try stopping
let the choir take a breath
we all grew thumbs once

Pocket Aliens

(for this poem to work, please imagine a world where we were invaded by tiny aliens who then lived in our pockets and told us to grow up.)

i
the clouds were ash
but she smiled when
there were strawberries
it can't be dark again

ii
when i touched her skin, my eyes drowned in river mist, or maybe a chemical mist that showers our corn and grain, or at least how it did before the aliens came to help.

help by setting us straight after an asteroid passed by their home planet and it made them look our way.

our way they watched a growing cloud of car exhaust, coastal floods and sloshing socks, the widening of hurricanes, millions of kids orphaned to AIDS, milk money locked in banks, and the dying of the dinosaurs on the dinosaurs' last ash-filled day.

iii
but a woman is no beacon
they do not burn the same
as dry wood

dry wood helped the pocket aliens find our little planet. it was during a time when i was alone in east tennessee, a time when i used to drink.

i used to drink hard root beer, and a lot of it. they're dangerous because you don't taste the alcohol. after many bottles, i sat in an old shed on the engine of a push lawn mower. summer sun shot needles through gaps in the dry-rotted boards. the gas cans were open. i lit matches over them and watched the flames crawl toward my fingertips.

my fingertips then gripped surplus red crayons from an olive garden, roma tomato red. i wrote letters to god on musty cardboard, waiting for the wax to dry. earlier, i had melted down a bulk of crayons and poured them into a 32-oz foam cup. for the wick, i cut my underwear into strips and braided a little rope. i dipped the wick into a clear liquid that rose to the top of a really old can of deck stain.

deck stain contains acetone, maybe. who knows? when the wax dried, i lit the candle. the crayon wax melted, and their oils floated to the top.

the top caught fire, and so did the cup, in the room filled with gas cans and dry wood. what a blaze! what a blaze!

iv
she stopped finding me at parties though i stood so near the ripest strawberries.

the ripest strawberries exist for a single moment before the ripeness fades away. this is the wisdom of my pocket alien, little and green, whispering in my ear, don't indulge too quickly, don't indulge too late, it's time to grow up.

it's time to grow up is what they came to say, squeaking it through their furry teeth. with all their technology, fast and sleek to streak across the galaxies, it's all they say.

they say it to the bankers bathing in soap suds and beggar pennies, those millions of evil men who cut their throats on diamonds and whiskey that fund entire countries where the presidents and prime ministers prop meager shoulders under an iron yoke loaded with cotton bales and backwoods handshakes. they sleep balled-up, with foreheads to their chests, listening to the pocket aliens whispering it's time to grow up.

it's time to grow up, sappy-sage millennials bitching about politics with the
ego of angels, bragging on instagram the whiteness of your feathered
wings. meanwhile your ethics are so carved in marble you wouldn't vote for
hillary in 2016. but where were your ears in 2022 to hear the crying of poor
women? can you connect the two? so ask the pocket aliens. it's time to
grow up.

it's time to grow up. i can hear their squeaky voices saying it, pinging pins
in my ears. poet boy! only children need a woman's lap to sleep! your peers
need people to stack stones that can hold up a roof when it rains. shred the
pillows and teddy bears, forget the bitches. sleep on wood or stone and
sober up for the day!

v
the clouds were ash
but she smiled when
there were strawberries
it can't be dark again
when i touched her skin
my eyes drowned
in river mist
but a woman is no beacon
they do not burn the same
she stopped finding me
at parties though
i stood so near
the ripest strawberries

in worlds governed by
economics

Gummy Bears

knock-knock—hello
we're here for gummy bears and salvation
our world is at war, and we're scared
we need rest and hydration

on the doorstep of a christian church, an alien family, little and round,
smiled at pastor bob. their purple skin was plump and squished in at the
touch. their sides bulged like a bunch of jelly was ready to burst out. they
all wore wire-framed glasses with two-inch-thick lenses. even the two kids
and the little tiny baby wore glasses. the little tiny baby looked like a
blueberry.

as the wind blew, the liquid inside made their skin ripple. the aliens smiled
through it.

knock-knock—hello
we're here for gummy bears and salvation
they took our home, now it's theirs
we need rest and hydration

pastor bob was almost bald. he was watering plants when the aliens
knocked. earlier that morning, while his freckled wife was still asleep,
pastor bob sat on the toilet. he stretched the skin on the back of one hand
so his wrinkles disappeared, just for a moment. at breakfast, he ate dry
cereal with coffee and quietly jotted in his prayer journal:

>*god, please impart on our congregation the spirit of generosity so we may build a new
sanctuary.*

knock-knock—hello
we're here for gummy bears and salvation
it's cold in this thin air
we need rest and hydration

the little aliens' home planet almost exclusively grew corn. it was basically
corn. the red kernels grew individually on vines instead of cobs. most of
the economy was based on extracting their syrup. the little jelly aliens
sustained themselves by filling up their plump bodies with the sticky liquid.

in a neighboring galaxy, a planet's inhabitants had eight limbs, each with a
spiny pincer on the end. their bodies were covered in long, yellow feathers
and spindly whiskers. the pincer-people considered the corn syrup a
delicacy, so they put on their atmosphere masks and traveled to the planet's
vineyards. in a matter of days, they popped half the population like grapes
in their pincers.

knock-knock—hello
we're here for gummy bears and salvation
may we please come upstairs
we need rest and hydration

Space Dragons

billionaires blasted their boner rockets
    and now they ain't
        the biggest bitches in space
           'cuz space dragons
               own the banks

        you ever call a credit card company
        but they forgot you owe them money?
        'n' you say, that's great 'cuz i'm poor
        but a new bill comes anyway?

space dragons clocked the rockets
and called our credit

     said they lent the blueprints to the egyptians
        now they're repo-ing the pyramids
        collect'n' on interest
           in crude oil and treasure

        you see
        space dragons
        hoard the cheese
        collapse economies
        in every galaxy
        blame it all
        on the people's
        democracy

the pimpled moon men
                tried to warn us
            sent us a tip
            told us space dragons
have a reputation
for capitol prediation

            they always take
                the prime real estate
                            mountains
                                    islands
                                        lakes

        earthly governments responded by declaring war
                and amazon trucks delivered
                    a box of flame throwers
            to every household, middle-class or poor
                            with a free netflix subscription
                            and pamphlets about patriotism

                the fire didn't even tinge their scales
                next thing you know
                they had them a real estate sale

space dragons took all the beach houses
and the rich had to vacate
        now billionaires ain't
            even affording
            a tent on a cheese rock

            but me and mine
                    we got took in
            by some good-hearted moon men
                    who can pay dragons some rent
                            we got our tent

a tent on a cheese rock
that ain't that bad
        plenty of space!

for a bed and a propane burner
and a cooler that fits a dozen eggs

we can live on that
we can live on that
        a bed and some eggs
        that ain't that bad

        so, let the dragons fly!
        let the space dragons drown in interest
        who says they gotta be slain?
        who's gonna do all that slaying
                                anyway?

                        you gonna do it?
                        you gonna do it
                        for just one more egg?

Alien Tea

i

juice helped us forget the smoke. every afternoon, teachers would gather us on the relentlessly-vacuumed carpet squares. us children, some still too young to read, sat cross-legged and stuck out our little pinkies. we sipped the juice and called it tea.

the school taught us to say "fog" instead of "smoke." they taught us that soy is a complete protein. we learned in chemistry that fog is just water, small and floating. i learned on a farm that soy bean farmers kill honey bees.

the smoke mixed with volcanic fumes, a puffy, white haze with silver flakes. it itched in our ears. based on income, we breathed in the smoke without filter. no one in town had air we could take, and our mothers taught us to share, anyway. and the government, blessed be they, distributed the tea for free.

we drank it with the gamy meat our parents killed illegally. it was so numbing to our noses and throats. the honor of hunting still ends with bloody lungs and shattered bones.

when my friends coughed, we sang about jesus and broke stale crackers in half. we washed them down with more tea. growing the wheat killed millions of field mice.

there had been no war in half a century. the prime minister was so proud that we celebrated once a year with charcoal, adding to the smoke. an army of uncles across the land donned stained aprons. they flipped pork steaks on miles of slated grills. this holiday slaughtered generations of smiling pigs.

ii

when it was time for us to come of age, we asked the big question. where do they get the tea?

we go! we go! we go to find the tea!

the man told us to climb the mountain. he told us through toothless gums, while sat in mildew and gray grit, the floor boards of a wilting home.

into the smoke, we trekked up a trail that cut over the ledge of a cliff. the smoke was so thick you'd think it was a wall, a white wall on the side of heaven, cloaking a sheer drop, hundreds of feet to the bottom. we passed between the wall on our right and the jungle on our left. it was infested with ferns and banana trees, wild ginger with pink flowers, lava rock and mud, spider webs wet and dripping. we walked as the spider silk caked our elbows. birds landed on coffee trees, and we flinched as the giant blobs of water, icy droplets, splashed on the backs of our necks. higher, the jungle grew chain link and concrete culvers. we passed, waist-deep, through spine-chilling water, abandoned irrigation channels, all the way to the top. the gate wasn't locked.

leaving our soaked outer clothes hanging on a fence, we continued in only our underwear. we huddled so the goose bumps on our shoulders rubbed against each other's, and walked through the gate to see where the tea got made.

light pins streamed through palm leaves and holes in the ceiling. squid tentacle dairy tubes tangled all across the warehouse, and the hum of oily pumps buzzed off corrugated metal.

iii

it was an alien attached to the tubes. the last one, maybe. massive and bound to iron I-beam pillars by hundreds of ratcheting canvas straps. we saw all her breasts clamped in silicon milking claws.

i apologized for not bringing knives. she laughed and told us to go home. we argued the justice from our textbooks. if we rally, she might go free.

"children of worms," she thundered, sultry like fingernails on velvet, "stop playing house. your lives have always meant killing."

in a world where aliens
invaded

Notes From Invasion
Fourth Revolution of the New Age

Introduction

Should this not be the twilight of humanity, and there are future babes to be born who are so inclined to study this period of history, I have taken it upon myself to document the public reaction from the first days of invasion. Due to my own limitations, both linguistically and technologically, I am left to transcribe oral accounts, online articles, and social media posts in the English language. I've arranged them in chronological order to the best of my ability.

Ships Landing

Holy Fuck! Aliens! Fuuuuuuuuuuuuuuuuuuuuuuuuuuck!
—Twitter post from a man in his twenties wearing a backwards-facing baseball hat

Breaking: Extraterrestrial crafts landing in major cities around the globe. No reports of anything exiting the crafts.
—Twitter, NBC News

Alright sheeple! Are you telling me it's a coincidence that these aliens just show up all the suddn on the anniversory of 2 days b4 the Kennedy Assassination, the VERY DAY Kennedy was in a hushed meeting with the Ford moter company and was threatened to not put the top DOWN????????Do your research!
—Facebook post by a history teacher at a private Baptist school in Missouri

I told you we shouldn't have sent our address into space…

On November 20th, 2022, aliens descended in their shimmering spaceships all across the planet. Reports indicate that every major city on Earth has received multiple ships, and thousands more landed in rural areas. With each landing, the earth shook with the intensity of an earthquake.

Monica Boil was at home when a ship landed just half a mile from her home in Little Rock, Arkansas. The hardwood floors rolled under Monica's feet where she was preparing dinner for the family of five. Pictures fell off the wall, chairs tipped over, and her young children, ages twelve, five, and three, hid under their beds. Monica had just poured juice into their cups, and it spilled all over the kitchen table and floor. Luckily, Monica had just purchased a six-pack of Bounty paper towels. Once the children were safe with their father in the master bedroom, she began soaking up the spilled juice with the extremely absorbent towels. It was the only thing that brought her a sense of normalcy and comfort.

We have no way of knowing how many more ships will land. In a world invaded by aliens, Bounty is here to keep your home from being invaded by mess.
—*Online article sponsored by Bounty*

We should bomb them. Get them the fuck off our world.
—*Twitter post from a fourteen-year-old with an anime character in their thumbnail*

Any bar that's around now never really closed. The ones that did were looted and never able to reopen. A few years after the debacle, I was having a drink. I had spent the morning laboring for our alien overlords and the afternoon reading. (They only make us work four hours, three days a week while they get more robots up and running, and only people aged 16 to 40, but not if they are pregnant or disabled. All things considered, they're not bad overlords.) A drunk man, inexplicably wearing flannel on a hot summer night, hung on my shoulder and told me this story:

"So when the first ships came down, I'm not gonna lie to you, I'm not gonna lie. I was fucking my neighbor's wife. I lost my job, it was a bad time, don't judge me! So I was fucking her real good, right? Real, real good and she was grunting and cussing and screaming my name and her hips were uuumph uuumph uuumph, ya know, and it felt so good, and boom! The ground just started shaking. And no shitting you, no shitting you, I came at that exact moment. I fi-I filled her all the way up. She was all screaming and shit. And boom! The sound! Re-remember-remember the sound? Boom, and the ground shook harder, and she screamed again. A second there, for asecond there, I thought...I thought I blew up her pussy with my en-en-enormous… cock."

After finishing his story, the man peed his pants and cried for fifteen minutes.
—Story later recounted to me at a bar three years after the ships landed

First Contact

Breaking: 1st sighting of aliens. Extremely tall, approx. 10–18 feet. Gray, light pink and light blue-colored beings have been spotted. No reports of contact.
—Twitter, NBC News

Alright, I don't know if you aliens use this website, but there was one of you, and we touched today. We were at the Raleigh's Grocery Store on Main. I know it sounds crazy, but you looked me in the eyes with your giant blue eyes (some people think it's weird, but I think it's freaking hot!) and ya know, I just can't stop thinking about you. You looked at me for a good few seconds, and I just really want to see you again. I'll be at 1756 Marshal Street, Apt 52, every night, with the curfew and what not. Please come over.
—Craigslist, lost connection posting

Welcome them and embody love
(further down)
They're not aliens! They are horsemen! REPENT!!!
(further down and to the right)
BOOBS
—*Vandalism on a bathroom mirror in my local grocery store*

Breaking: Alien seen clearing path by tossing parked pickup truck off road with only one hand.
—*Twitter, NBC News*

I know we got aliens now, but you're the only one I see that's out of this world!
—*Tinder message shown to me by a female friend*

Breaking: Washington D.C., aliens approached by diplomats and military officials. Aliens sat cross-legged in a semi-circle and tried to hold hands. U.S. officials refused.
—*Twitter, NBC News*

What if they're nice?
—*Twitter post by a scientist with a TV show*

We don't really know why the aliens came, but when they got here to Lincoln, they ate all the biscotti. And I mean ALL of it. More actually had to be made! Wild, right?

There's an Italian couple in Lincoln, and I've heard stories that they wept with joy when the orders started coming in. Of course, the aliens don't pay for shit, they just take. Still, for the first time since I've been alive, the baristas weren't about to open without a full jar of FUCKING BISCOTTI! I saw one alien crunching on the cookie-from-a-time-before-we-discovered-what-makes-a-cookie-a-cookie in their big, metallic molars.

The Italian couple bakes all the biscotti in Lincoln, which means they used to fire up the oven maybe three times a year, tops. I'm willing to bet no one had actually eaten their biscotti in at least a decade. It always just sat in those glass jars at the coffee shops for three to four months, uneaten. At that point, the extra rock-hard biscotti was thrown out, and the Italian couple received an order to make more.

Now, their ovens are PUMPING! I'm amazed they haven't died of exhaustion. These aliens are crazy—they just LOVE it.
—Blog post from someone in Lincoln, Nebraska

Conflict

Breaking: Multiple attacks on aliens from around the globe. Many aliens reported injured. No deaths.
—Twitter, NBC News

Stop shooting them! We don't know what they will do!
—Twitter post from a rapper

In these uncertain times, I think of my children. I think of the world I worked so hard to create for them. I think of all the things they might not get to do. Will they finish college? Will they even get to have a family of their own? Will they buy a house? Will they land their dream job? Please pray for the children.
—Facebook post from a middle-aged white woman posted with a picture that showed a lot of cleavage

Breaking: Alien ship bombed in Yemen. U.S. involvement speculated.
—Twitter, NBC News

Can we chill?
—Twitter post by a high school dropout

The fact that these aliens don't have penises just shows that the patriarchy is not a universal norm.
—Twitter post by a person with purple hair and a lot of face piercings

Breaking: In a coordinated effort, aliens approached heads of state in every nation on Sunday morning.
—Twitter, NBC News

Goddamnit! They're at the WHITE house. It's like a horror movie. The WHITE president and WHITE cabinet are about to howdy-do our species into extinction!
—Text message from a group chat on a cell phone I found

Breaking: Ongoing talks with aliens around globe. Some friendly, some hostile.
—Twitter, NBC News

Breaking: Inside source reveals several diplomats insisted on seeing the aliens' flag. Spent forty minutes attempting to explain the concept of flags and nations.
—Twitter, NBC News

wyd
—Tinder message shown to me by a female friend

Breaking: Aliens killed! Reports of targeted alien attacks in Russia, China, North Korea, U.S., Turkey and Egypt.
—Twitter, NBC News

Pray
—Twitter post by a retired army general

The Defeat

"So, when the attacks happened, I wanted to show them it's not all of us, you know? And I thought, well, what do I have that is like, peaceful, right? And then I remembered I have all my My Little Ponies in a closet. Not the closet in my bedroom, but the closet by the kitchen. It's smaller, but my bedroom closet is just SO full of clothes. I have so many that I just can't get rid of, so there's just no room. So all my linens and other extra stuff, ya know, like stuff you don't always need, like you only need sometimes, like maybe once a year? Like, for instance, I have a screwdriver in there. Not the drink, but, like, the metal thing to put the screws in IKEA stuff, because, like, the tools IKEA gives you hurt your fingers and chip nails and I ALWAYS realize I need something from IKEA immediately after getting my nails done, and men, MEN are just useless. They come over and want to put it together for me, and I try to let them…and they get mad…and they grunt and they can't do it, but then they still want to have sex, and it's like, you can't even assemble a bookshelf with the instructions…it's like, you are NOT attractive to me right now. So anyway, what were we talking about? Oh yeah, so I got my favorite My Little Pony out and I carried it outside. It was a little cold, and I forgot my jacket, but I didn't go back in because I was afraid of chickening out. So, I walked down to the coffee shop on my street, and there's always an alien there sitting on the patio sipping coffee. And he looked so funny because he was SO big! He looked like an adult sitting at a little kids table with his knees raised up super high. So, I walked up to his table with my My Little Pony, put it on his table, and smiled. And it was SO cute! He smiled back at me SO big! And he took the My Little Pony and held it in his lap while he finished the coffee!"

—Story told to me by a 23-year-old woman who wore her hair in pig tails

Breaking: NO MORE LEADERS. Aliens executed all heads of state overnight by twisting heads off their bodies. Seized world-wide control.

—Twitter, NBC News

When I was younger I worked in a barbecue restaurant in West Louisiana. I was the only white person working there and faced daily discrimination. That experience taught me what it's like to be African American, and since then, I've stood in solidarity with them. Now that the aliens are taking our homes, I feel like this experience is happening to me all over again, but this time I understand what it is to be Native American. I feel empathy for them now on a level that I've never felt before. Of course, it was just human nature, and we did it to them before they did it to us, and I don't have any control over that. Now I think it's time to leave all of that in the past, because this is bigger than the differences between people. We are under attack, and we have to come together to protect our families, our property, and our FREEDOM!!

—Facebook post posted with a picture of an American flag

Bet you wish you didn't ghost me now! Bitch! I'll be drinking beer in my bunker!
(one hour later)
Hey, I was just kidding. Do you want the address to my bunker?
(one hour later)
1515 North Highway 79. Knock on the steel door in the back.
{UFO emoji} {eggplant emoji}
(15 minutes later, he sent a dick pic)

—Tinder message shown to me by a female friend

Final Thoughts

The websites were all taken down when the aliens took control. These brief comments are all I could gather in a short window of time, years ago now. I haven't touched this since then, but wanted to organize them on paper, and add a few things I saw or heard along the way, before it's too late.

There's rebellion in the air. There will be war. Again.

We Grew Up Skinny Dipping
Seventy-Eighth Revolution of the New Age

1

in our childhood summer, noontime clouds brought a mugginess that
dripped wet sand. the sand piled on the second hand of our clock. it turned
the ticks into thuds, and then into the bass of a drum. on those days, we
ran barefoot under pine trees and through floating screens of gnats. at the
pond, we skinny dipped. my friends were too heavy to swim and waded in
the shallows. i treaded further, and dove between the legs of bow-legged
skeletons.

the grown-ups said there had been a war.

2

today i'm at a beach, the northern beach molded from cliffs and pebbles. i
came alone. a lot of life is alone. am i cool for saying it?

in the rocks, i built a fire. the flames climbed with a pharaoh's ego,
whipping-whipping smoke into the air—a pillar—a pyramid—a grave.
some of my relatives cling to permanence that way. they still save to buy
burial markers, even on a remote, country planet like ours.

when the fire babbled into the spluttering dementia of dying kings,
popping against the black crumble of shriveled logs, only then i added
wood. who wants to collect more?

3

my alien friends had thick, stone-like fingertips at the end of long digits, six
on each hand. they grew much faster than i did and shot up to twelve-feet-
tall by the time we were ten years old. their bodies turned spindly, like the
dying branches of juniper trees. they took their giant strides slowly so i
could keep up.

my friends were kind. angels bubbled from their bass voices to stroke the
backs of my species' grandmothers, whose husbands died in the war or
from the war. grandmothers can't help but love all children.

my friends were warm. they had skin that felt like candle wax a minute after
the wick was blown to smoke. i would sleep with my ear nuzzled in the
crooks of their arms.

4

i'm cooking sausage and sipping whiskey. grandpa told me we are lucky to
still have so much sausage. every farmer i've worked for raises pigs. no one
really tries to domesticate the wild cattle anymore. my grandpa may have
been the last one. i miss his steaks. he cut them two inches thick.

i have two knives for utensils. i thrust them through the casing, bursting
boiling juice into the angry flames as i flip the meat on the grill. one blade
is cheap, stainless steel—a pocket knife i found in an abandoned car. the
other is immaculate—a thick, curved knife with an oak and epoxy handle.
some rust spots show its age. grandpa made it from an old chainsaw bar.
there's no more gas to run chainsaws anyway.

many have told me i'm someone who could lead. they use words like
"rebuild."

5

i've given kerosene and cloth to a government built from shambled match heads. our economy barters or burns.

despite their promises, i will not give my time.

my time is given to river pebbles trapped between exposed tree roots, kneeling and pinching them in my fingers.

my time is given to sacks of grain, throwing them for a dinner from the farmers table.

my time is given to dead sleep in early evenings, because there are no dreams until morning. in my dreams, my rock pillows turn soft, and me and my friends inherit a kingdom everlasting, a kingdom of coffee steam.

in spite of the calluses, my hands are soft. women comment how much they love that before they leave.

i saturate my blood in canned caffeine and carry rocks to build mountains.

at least the clouds will touch my grave.

i haven't cried a sober tear since i was fifteen.

and i still haven't showered since i fucked that girl on sunday.

6

each one of my friends had soft, bulbous eyes, sapphire blue you could
almost smell. in their youth, they shed big, blobby tears every sunset. the
aliens have short life spans. at least they are short on our planet. their waxy
skin dries and starts cracking by the time they are twelve or thirteen.

7

there is a family of giants camping next to me. they spent the day making
graham crackers on the fire. my grandpa did that for me once.

one parent snuck away after dinner and then returned with wax-paper
morsels. the children hounded her, forcing their bugging, blue eyes over
her elbows. she unwrapped the packages, revealing the dark brown
chocolate blocks and cream squares of marshmallow. grandpa said they
used to be common, but now not many people remember how to make the
candies.

the family made s'mores.

dammit! there must be a part of me that wants a family.

8

my friends and i shared a play room. our moms watched us with one eye.

the other eye was always bedded down in slumbering grass, following the
carbon storm—the burnt fields and uprooted carrots—the mold in winter
bread—the worms in salted pork—the dying of chickens, and the tumors
we find in their livers—the times without rain.

we played on our bellies. our moms took turns tickling toddler armpits.

9

my grandpa told me it's important that i find a woman (and maybe three or
four) to keep the species going.

burn the boats!

burn down the firewood and sleep in the cold! the whiskey is low—less
than a third sloshing in the bottle.

10

i see them playing, the children. my friends are their ancestors, now
generations back. the ones here, too, will be with the dust, so soon. so
soon.

though i am history, i do not engage. i am hieroglyphs in skin, the keeper of
generations, the song of times forgotten. i am a god to them, all knowing
with my toes planted in the dirt. i am the answer to that alien prayer, i want
to know god or the earth! i am silent.

11

before i was sixteen, i only had one friend left. she had no children of her
own. her eyes were shrunken and the color of dusty sea shells. my friend
rested her massive, gangly hand on my knee and sunk with creaking bones
into the alien planet.

12

into the ocean! into the ocean! i walk with two knives, the sharp blades
brushing my knees, slicing. my bare feet press and part the icy salt, foaming
tide, bubbles catching in leg hair.

an empty whiskey bottle sits at the tent of aliens. it's the only bible they get.

back to primordial! forget the stars! burn like summer underbrush. die in a
flash. warm the earth for ant pupae. warm the ponds for dragonfly larva!

give your breath to our wind, alien children! let them mix and carry barley
seeds to new planes. walk with our deer, and let us die away.

13
blue-eyed child, you cannot swim. your skinny body is just too heavy.

blue-eyed child with marshmallow on your waxy lips. i am too deep. your arms are not as long as you think.

blue-eyed child. my hand is crushed in yours. i can see your chin, now, from under the green water. i've lost my knives.

blue-eyed child, why are you pulling me back?

At heart, Kory is a bum. His greatest wish is to lay around on hay bales, sip cappuccinos, watch anime, and wonder about monsters or aliens or women. In his paradise, he would never actually endure the toil of writing. However, some dastardly force, whether random evolution or cosmic power, has infected the poet with a torturous amount of ambition. And so, instead of handing his life over to chips and salsa on feathered pillows, Kory spends his days pursuing a small pack of goals that dart and zig like frightened squirrels. He writes poems and stories about aliens, monsters, the apocalypse, society, love, and lust. Kory is also a professional in affordable housing and passionate about alleviating the current crisis. Additionally, to balance the creative and social with the physical, he trains for and competes in the sport of amateur strongman.

Kory's poetry has appeared in several journals. He is a regular performer at Sacramento's legendary event, Joe Montoya's Poetry Unplugged. The poet also leads a small workshop with some of Sacramento's best writers, and, from time to time, performs one-man shows.

Ambition is a hell of a thing. If it could be squeezed out of Kory's bones— just rung out like a rag—and captured in jelly jars, Kory would plop them clanking in a grain sack and re-gift the whole lot on a holiday.

Website: koryvance.com
Instagram: @strength_and_poetry